How To Help Your Child Get Better Grades Easier

Powerful Interactive Strategies Designed to Pinpoint and Eliminate Barriers to Your Child's Academic Success

Selina Jackson, M.A.

Acknowledgements

Thanks to:

Dr. Kembleton Wiggins, Ph.D, Ed.D, my friend, colleague, and mentor. I appreciate that you continually encourage me to pursue the dream. Without whom, I would never have done it.

All of the educators that I have worked with over the years who helped to spark the ideas. Their experience, feedback, and professional knowledge was invaluable.

The students that I have worked with over the years; those who allowed me to experiment and explore the many ways to improve student learning and success. Their patience, cooperation, and most of all, sense of humor helped to keep us all among the sane.

Table Of Contents

INTRODUCTION:
Why is School Success Such a Problem?

In order to be successful in school, students are required to master certain skills and concepts. But for some, it's a never-ending battle just to get there. From their perspective, they wake up five days a week, too early, leave home sleepy, hungry, possibly feeling irritated and grumpy just to face a multitude of tasks that seemingly have no value, no importance, and no connection with what they face daily in their personal lives.

They also have to deal with those peers who use bully tactics, charisma, money, looks, and whatever else is available to them, to manipulate and control.

And let's not forget to mention the almighty math problems... *problems*; the name in and of itself suggests something else to avoid at all costs. *(Who needs more problems anyway?)* No wonder many students would rather turn their backs, clown around, and pretend it just isn't so. Won't it be a relief when we find a way to help them get past the barriers to their success?

Five Levels of Commitment

1. I'll think about it.
2. I'll try.
3. I'll do what I can.
4. I'll do what's expected.
5. I'll do whatever it takes

This book, a product of Super Achievement, Inc., is a study of what works. It is based on Neuro-Linguistic Programming (NLP) and studies the way we process information through our senses of sight, hearing, touch, smell, and taste, how we use language, and describes the specific steps we take to achieve what we want to achieve. In the early

1970's, Richard Bandler and John Grinder, original co-developers, did much to develop this revolutionary approach to the human experience. They taught people how to go beyond the verbal, to use non-verbal cues to develop effective communication and to bring about quick behavioral change.

Super Achievement... also utilizes the findings in Brain-based Learning Research, which supports the importance of helping students to tap into and develop both of the brain's hemispheres in order to achieve optimum learning.

Studies of the brain show that we need to move, sing, dance, draw, discuss and reflect to learn effectively. As we grow up and attend school, we are constantly being told to be quiet, sit still, stop daydreaming, stop doodling, and pay attention. For the child who *sees the light* best by drawing diagrams and symbols, or the child that grasps what's being presented best by moving around, or the verbal child who needs to discuss ideas to understand, we have taken away their most effective modes for learning.

a. How This Book Works For You

This book focuses on ways to increase your awareness of, management, and *acceleration* of your child's *thinking, learning, and communication (TLC) style*. There are assessments and activities that are designed to help you discover how your child learns easiest and best. Why is this important?

Research shows that in order for students to learn more effectively, instruction needs to be varied and geared to multiple styles of learning. Thomas Armstrong, Ph.D., (In Their Own Way, 2000), supports a "varied teaching repertoire." By doing this, he says, "I believe millions of so called learning disabled, ADHD, and underachieving youngsters would lose their disability and millions of other children would begin to realize more of their true potential."

Unfortunately, schools are *not* all doing what the research suggests. Classrooms are *not* all student-centered, and teachers are *not* all using a variety of instructional strategies. This could be why your child has lost interest and may *not* be performing academically at his or her best.

Does he look interested to you? ⟶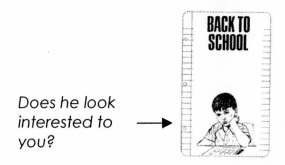

What if you had some powerful techniques in your box of tricks that could assist you in helping your child **learn faster**, **easier** and **more enjoyably**? Would knowing how to do that bring your goals even closer? Just think of what you could accomplish! Not to mention the needless trouble you can avoid.

The information in this book will give you a strong start. Try it for yourself and you'll be able to decide how best to use it to achieve exactly what you want to achieve and I'm sure others will notice your efforts.

b. The Easier Process

John went to a psychiatrist and said, "Doc, I got issues. Every time I get in bed, I imagine there's somebody under it. I get under the bed and I feel there's somebody on top of it. Top, under, top, under. I'm going crazy."

"Just let me work with you for two years." the doctor said. "See me three times a week, and I'll cure you."

"What's does it cost?" John asked. "$75 a session." "I'll consider it." John replied.

John didn't see the shrink until six months later at the car wash. "Why didn't you ever come see me again?" "For $75 bucks a visit? A bartender cured me for $7."

"What? How'd he do that?" the doc asked.

"He told me to *cut the legs off the bed!*"

c. Process vs. Content

Typically, especially in education, the focus has been primarily on *content* (the *what*). Students need to know *this* information and students need to know *that standard*. The problem is much of the content that we're presenting, many students just aren't getting. They are having a difficult time hearing what we are say, they're just not seeing the whole picture. It's not that they can't learn what is required, it's that many just don't know how. When they lack the "know how" of the "process" of learning, they're fooled into thinking that spelling is hard, reading is difficult, and math is pretty much impossible. Imagine what could happen when students develop a "how-to" system, a process for learning that will enable them to learn anything faster, easier and more enjoyably. This book will help you show them how, but in a compellingly creative and educational way.

TLC Tips:

- ❑ provide hints on how to *apply the concept to your child*.
- ❑ are designed to help your child strengthen the use of all learning modalities.
- ❑ give you insight and experience into helping your child succeed faster, easier, and more enjoyably.

Picture this: your child becomes even more responsible for his or her own behavior and education. Is this something that you can benefit from? What problems will you avoid when (s)he does? Well, the pages in this book are designed to help. Haven't you waited long enough to get what you want?

1. What's The Meaning Of This?

Ever walked away from a conversation wondering, "What in the world *was* she talking about?" Or, after a somewhat heated dialogue with your mate, feeling like, "He just *doesn't* understand..." Maybe you've clashed with your teen and countered, "I *wish* you would try and see it from my perspective."

Most of us have, at one time or another experienced misunderstandings and conflicts at our jobs and in our relationships. Did you know that most of those little unnerving, stressful scenarios can be avoided when we understand and utilize the secrets behind a few simple principles.

1. We experience the world through our senses.
2. We experience the world differently.
3. Meaning is in people and not in words.

Dr. K.S. Wiggins, Social Psychologist says, "90% of all conflict stems from a problem with definitions". Consider the implications of that.

"An anecdote is a tale," the teacher explains.
"Now, Maria use it in a sentence."
I tied a tin cup to the dog's *anecdote*."

a. Why is Meaning in People and Not in Words?

A person uses his senses to take in, process, and give out information. Three of the five senses, eyes (visual), ears, (auditory), and the sense of touch, or feeling (kinesthetic), we use, primarily to perceive, store and retrieve data helpful to us in our relationships, and professional lives.

Even though we use all three, we may process information better and more quickly in one of the senses. That would be considered the "dominate processing modality." This modality (sense) through which we think, learn, and communicate most frequently is referred to as our TLC style. We tend to interpret data and perceive the world around us according to our unique style.

Did you know that your child's TLC style could be the reason why your child isn't performing at his best? By uncovering, and eliminating the subconscious issues and mixed messages that could prevent your child from operating at peak efficiency, you can *achieve* more, faster and easier, have *greater creativity*, *more energy*, and *eliminate headaches* no matter what the task. And you know this will benefit you immediately!

2. TLC Styles – What's Your Child's?

a. How Your Child Thinks, Learns, and Communicates

As babies, we learn very rapidly though the use all of our senses. As we grow older we continue to experience and learn about the world around us through them. But, usually over time a preference for one sensory system develops and tends to dominate.

If a person has a predominately **visual** style or preference (referred to as a visual) he uses more of the visual strategies (pictures and images) for processing information. Those who learn or remember best what they hear or discuss, prefer an **auditory** style of processing information. The **Kinesthetics** are those students who prefer to touch and feel in order to process information. Often, in the classroom, they are the ones who get up fifteen times to sharpen their *ink pens!*

Q & A: Ink pens? Do we now have ink pens that you can sharpen?

I haven't heard of any. But see, that's the whole point. Since Kinesthetics *have* to move, touch, and feel in order to process information, if they are not given the opportunity to do so, they'll *create* their own reasons to move.

They'll ask to go to the bathroom over and over, and put their hands, feet, and other body parts on anything or anyone in their paths. They'll break the lead on their pencil countless number of times, and oh, and if you're not directly in their path? No problem. They'll get to you. They seem to specialize in mixing movement with speed.

They can cover the distance of the entire room within a few moments. Encircling, encroaching, and hovering over any warm bodies... they will invite themselves into your space. And when all else fails, they will invariably get themselves "kicked-out"... and then the negative information comes your way.

What if there was some way you could go into the busy mind of that child and discover just what makes him tick? Do you think that would make it easier to get him to do what you want? Certainly! When you recognize and utilize your child's dominant TLC style, it will open the door to unlimited possibilities and show you the right way to get there.

"*I did it my way...*" the singer croons feelings of pride, satisfaction, and accomplishment. When students use their own built-in tools and strategies to meet academic challenges successfully, we all win. Well, now it makes even more ***sense*** to get a grasp on how each child's mind works to process information.

b. Reading Your Child's Mind

What if you really could read your child's mind? Imagine what insight you could gain, and how much easier it would be for you to get whatever it is that you really want...Think it's possible? Well, before you toss the possibility aside, consider this:

One of the easiest ways to **tell** how a person thinks is to *listen* to the "predicates" or sensory specific words that a person is using. For example, a person thinking in pictures and images (visual) will use phrases like, "Oh, I *see*, Can you *show* me? Or, I now have a ***clear picture*** of what to do." A person who's thought pattern is auditory will say things like, "I *hear* you. Things are starting to *click*. Are you *listening*, etc? The person operating from a kinesthetic standpoint, says things like...I've ***got*** it! ***Give*** me a minute, will you? I have finally ***grasped*** this concept.

The bold, italicized words above indicate which of the five senses is being used to process, or communicate information at that particular time. These words are ***"sensory-specific."*** We use these and others in our thinking, learning, and communicating (TLC).

When it seems that someone doesn't understand what we say, we tend to feel annoyed, upset, and frustrated. Students, who don't perceive clearly what we are teaching them, experience those same kinds of feelings and more. Using words that match our student's internal processing system, their TLC style, will help us avoid needless stress and give us the advantage.

Did you know that by recognizing how another person processes information and by *matching* their TLC style, you can:

1. *Increase the attention* that they pay to you?
2. Decrease time used for trying to *get them to understand?*
3. Use words that *change minds and behavior?*

That means you can now save more of your energy for doing the things that you enjoy. *Now who doesn't want to do that?*

Selina Jackson, M.A.

Sensory Specific Language Chart

Visual	Auditory	Kinesthetic
I can *see* what it is.	I *hear* you.	I don't *get* it.
The *picture* is *clear*.	You're not *listening*.	Stay in *touch*.
Show me the money.	Money *talks*..	*Give* me the money.
Look at it from this *view*.	It's starting to *click*.	I *got a handle* on…
Visualize…	This *sounds* good.	I *feel* that we're…
We're *seeing eye-to-eye*.	We're in *tune*.	That's *cool*.

Question:
1. If you were to guess which is yours and your child(ren)'s dominate TLC style, which would you choose? Hint: Which words do you/they typically use?

Activity – (You'll need paper and pencil)
1. Interview your child(ren). Ask the following questions.
2. Get <u>three</u> answers and list them ***exactly*** the way they say them.
3. Go back and read their answers to discover which TLC style words dominate?

   a. *What do you (or don't you) like about the place where you live?*
   b. *What makes you happy?*
   c. *Describe the ideal vacation.*

- If your child uses the words in the ***"visual"*** box, he or she is thinking in pictures.
- If (s)he uses "hearing" ***(auditory)*** words, then (s)he is thinking in words.
- The other child who uses "feeling" or action words ***(kinesthetic),*** has to move*, touch, or feel in order to think.

*If your child's teacher is unaware of this important fact, this can cause your child and you a whole lot of needless problems. However, if your child's classroom is student-centered and a variety of teaching and learning strategies are present, it increases your child's chances of success.

TLC Tip:
When disciplining your child, *match the language* of the TLC style.

If your visual child says, I don't **see** why I have to..." and you counter with, "Because I **said** so." Did you match her style? No. Therefore, you may be in for a rude awakening (and we know how *alarming* those can be).

A more effective way is to **match the sensory language** that your child is using. This way they listen and follow your directions easier and more enjoyably.

Aw, Mom. I don't **see** why I have to do my homework right now.

Let me **show** you a couple of reasons.

Visuals:
- They will be convinced when they can *see* how doing it will benefit them.
- Paint a *clear picture* in your child's mind of the benefits as well as the consequences of certain behaviors.
- *Show* them how to do it successfully.

Then, you'll both see eye-to-eye and you'll avoid any unnecessary stress. The TLC Style Behavioral Chart (coming up) shows specific *behaviors* of each style. Read it and instantly realize why using old, burned-out methods of instruction has now outlived it's usefulness and effectiveness and there is no longer any need to do it.

At the Movies

Sensory-Specific Language is in our everyday life, even the music and movies we enjoy! Place a check in the TLC category(s) where each movie title fits. Identify the clue word(s). The first one has been done for you.

Movie	V	A	K	Clue Word(s)
1. **Dodge**ball			√	*Dodge*
2. Freedom **Song**				
3. Crazy **Beautiful**				
4. Look Who's Talking				
5. The Sound of Music				
6. Fear and Loathing in Las Vegas				
7. The Untouchables				
8. Beauty and the Beast				
9. Pitch Black				
10. Scream II				

C. TLC Style Behavioral Chart
(What Your Child's Behavior Means)

	KINESTHETIC	AUDITORY	VISUAL
Learns by:	doing, hands-on experiences.	hearing, lectures, discussions.	seeing, looking at demonstrations.
When inactive:	finds reasons to move.	hums, talks to self, drum on table,	stares, draws, watches something.
Remembers:	what was done.	verbals, names, rote memorization.	what was seen, faces, sight words.
Likes/needs:	action, movement, wiggling, space.	music, debates, the sound of his own voice.	movies, reading, staring into space, doodling.
Distracted by:	unfinished projects, inability to move.	sounds, noise.	visual disorder.
Shows emotions:	in body movement, muscle tone.	in tone and pitch of voice.	in facial expressions.
Posture/ movement:	repeats *random* movements, walks heel to toe, move first then look.	nodding head, repeats movement in a pattern.	straight back, chin down, still body and head, look first, then move
When pressured or stressed:	moves	talks	freezes
Relaxes by:	moving or being still.	being quiet, choosing what to listen to.	closing eyes, choosing what to look at.
The way their mind works:	doesn't like to plan, makes piles, looks down or away to think, gestures when speaking.	talks through things, spells phonetically, sub-vocalizes, enjoys hearing own voice.	likes to plan, things organized, files cabinets may even be color coded, makes lists.

TLC Tip:
Before speaking, get your Kinesthetic child's attention by moving in close (to his or her side) and/or putting your hand gently on his/her shoulder.

Since "K's" are more affected by movement and touch, often, they don't "get it" when you talk to them from across the room. Using proximity (closeness and position) to get their attention before you give them directions works faster.

Also, give them one or two directions at a time. It's easier. Have them pace or gesture while they tell you in their own words what they are to do. Then have them imagine themselves doing it. This will help them process the information easier.

> What are you going to do?

> First, I will hang up my clothes, then take out the trash.

Kinesthetics:

- Need to *get* a picture in their imaginations, to visualize themselves doing something successfully.
- Help them *grasp* the benefits they will get and the problems they will avoid by completing the task.
- You model for them and then have them model for you how to do it correctly.

Then they will finally grasp what you *really* mean when you say, "Clean up your room."

School Days Quiz

Think back to the time when you were in school. Recall your **worst** or **best** classroom experience. Answer the following questions.

1. What type of seating?
   a. desks in line
   b. tables
   c. other
      (list)_____

2. How did your teacher usually present information?
   a. lecture
   b. used handouts, overheads, videos
   c. set up an activity where you could discover the information for yourself.
   d. other_____

3. How long was a typical lecture?
   a. 5-10 minutes
   b. 11-15 minutes
   c. 16-20 minutes
   d. 21 or more

4. **While** the teacher lectured, the students were usually required to:
   a. sit still and listen
   b. take notes
   c. draw or doodle
   d. fill in missing information on a lecture sheet
   e. other_____

5. We worked in groups:
   a. 10% of the time or less
   b. 25% of the time
   c. 50% of the time
   d. 75% of the time

6. We learned new things by:
   a. reading, looking at pictures, demonstrations or movies.
   b. using music.
   c. using our hands and/or movement.
   d. other_____

7. We learned to spell by:
   a. looking *up* at words placed on the walls or
      ceiling, then visualizing them
   b. writing the words
   c. sounding the word out
   d. other_____

8. We reviewed or studied for a test by:
   a. acting out what we learned
   b. discussing, reciting, or debating what we learned
   c. writing answers down on paper
   d. other_____

9. What we learned was:
   a. always in some way connected to our everyday life
   b. usually in some way connected to our everyday life
   c. sometimes connected to our everyday life
   d. seldom connected to our everyday life
   e. never connected to our everyday life

10. The class in which I learned the most *more enjoyably* was:

   _____

11. What was it about this class that made learning fun?

   _____

12. Some say that most schools are set up for the **visual** TLC Style.
    Take another look at the visual side of the chart and notice how
    most of the characteristics listed are things that students must do in
    order to be successful in most schools. What did you discover?

   _____

13. In classrooms that are student-centered, lessons are structured to meet the needs of all students, and a wide variety of instructional strategies are used. In here, students usually learn faster, easier, and more enjoyably. Which of your classroom experiences do you believe was more student-centered?

_____

TLC Tip:
Teach your Auditory child how to repeat directions to himself and listen to her "inner" voice.

It is necessary for "A's" to talk and discuss in order to process information. They need to hear the teacher's words in their own voice. Auditories who haven't learned how to repeat directions *inside their heads*, will often say it aloud. They also may come across as the "Town Crier", telling everything they hear. We all know that kids who "talk too much" or at the wrong time, get in hot water.

Explain this to your kids and tell them to repeat something you've said "inside" their heads, and then repeat it to you. This will help them to avoid trouble in school.

In addition, often when the teacher is lecturing, Auditories will talk to their neighbors about subjects *seemingly* unrelated to the lesson. This is because they hear something that reminds them of an experience they had. They are verbally making the connection between the information the teacher is giving and their life. If teachers don't get that, and don't allow periodic moments of *"buzz time"*, then you just might get a note or phone call from the teacher saying your child is talking too much or disrupting the class.

Teach your child(ren) how to make their TLC style work for and not against them. Go on to the next section to find out how.

3. Practical Suggestions for Easier TLC Style Learning

a. WHO ARE YOU? (A Fun Personality Quiz)

If you could be any one of these shapes, which would you choose?

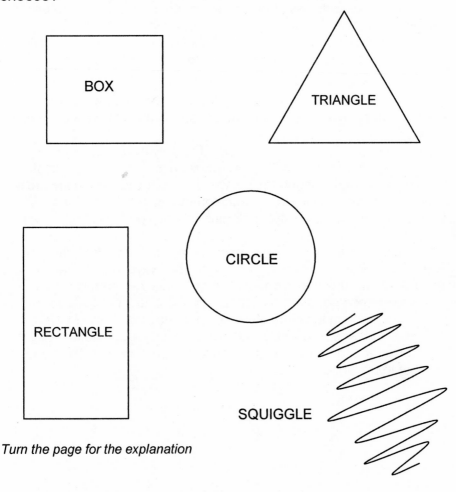

Turn the page for the explanation

WHO ARE YOU-Explanations

If you chose the box that means, you love the rules. You like things to be in order. You prefer to know what's coming BEFORE it gets here.

If your choice was, the triangle, that means that you are a leader. Yep, that's right. You were born that way. Leaders can't be chosen, they aren't elected, *they are born.*

The rectangle suggests that you don't know who you are right now. You are in transition (relax, it's only temporary).

Choosing the circle says that you are a "people person". You enjoy being with people, you usually get along well with others.

If your preference was the squiqqle, that means you hate the rules. You like to be spontaneous, go with the flow.

By doing this activity, we discover that just like we may not all choose the same shape, we will not all be motivated by the same things, and in a sense, we are NOT all created equal.

This strongly suggests that if we want to truly inspire our kids, and make our job easier, we won't always choose the *same old ways* of trying to get them to cooperate. We won't voice the same old ineffective "sermonettes" that usually begin with something like, *"How many times…?"* (You know the ones that your kids can probably recite, word for word).

No. Instead, we will use the principle of diversity to our advantage. We will find faster, easier, and more enjoyable ways to motivate them, especially as we use the powerful strategies this section has to offer.

The round-peg-square-hole concept is obsolete for today's youth. Trying to force them to fit into a pre-set mold has now outlived it's usefulness and effectiveness and there is no longer any need for us to do it. Consider and do the suggestions in this section now. Then you'll really get to understand.

b. Easier "A Style" Learning

"finely tuned ears"

appreciation of words, articulate

- Learns by hearing *AND* discussion.
- Has to talk in order to process information.
- May get in hot water for talking too much.

List several other characteristics of the Auditory TLC style? (Answers on the next page)

a. _____

b. _____

c. _____

Who does this remind you of?_____

AUDITORY LEARNERS: learn through listening *and talking*...

- These learners enjoy lectures *with discussion*, talking things through and listening to what others have to say. Auditories "hear" what you really mean in your tone, pitch, speed, etc., of your voice. They often benefit from reading aloud, using a tape recorder, or listening to books on tape.
- They are usually elegant speakers. They talk to themselves rather than create mental pictures.
- Although Auditories like to hear verbal instruction, they find it easier and more enjoyable to learn by repeating what's been said. They enjoy dialogues, discussions, plays, and love to debate. They often remember names and forget faces.
- They find solutions to problems by talking them through.
- Although they make noise, they are easily distracted by it and often will complete individual work easier when it is quiet.

So, for easier "A Style" learning:

- Discuss, recite, and debate what you learn.
- Make speeches and presentations.
- Use a tape recorder during lectures while taking notes. Rewrite your notes.
- Read your text out loud. You'll get more meaning.
- Create musical jingles and mnemonics to help you remember information.
- Dictate your ideas to someone while they write what you say.
- Tell a short story to demonstrate your point.
- Ask for discussion about any written information.
- Ask the teacher to explain diagrams, graphs and maps.
- Do a "group study" so you can explain information.

TLC TIP:
Encourage your child to find better ways to make a "boring"
class more enjoyable.

Often Auditories and Kinesthetics are quite entertaining. They say and do things that are funny. They tend to draw attention to themselves. Since Kinesthetics are action-orientated, they will provide the entertainment when they consider class boring. If teachers never allow students to connect their natural humor to the lesson, it could mean unnecessary trouble for your child.

It's true, sometimes classes are boring and lack connection to their everyday lives (especially if they aren't student-centered). So, I don't blame them for feeling the way they do. Explain to your child that you understand that, however, fooling around, cracking jokes, and entertaining while the teacher is trying to teach will eventually bring TOO MUCH ATTENTION and the wrong kind.

What are some of the things that can possibly happen if they don't find better ways to make their learning experience more enjoyable?

- They'll get watched like a hawk.
- They'll get blamed for things they didn't do.
- When the whole group is talking, *their* name will get called.
- Others may get more chances while they get referrals.
- They'll get into trouble for things that others don't.
- Their actions will be scrutinized and judged against them even if they meant well, and more...

Ask your child to tell you a few other possible consequences and if this is what (s)he really wants. (Probably not). Then, have your child come up with several things he or she can do to make their classroom experience a better one. There are some suggestions in the appendix that you or your child can share with the teacher as well.

c. **Easier "K Style" Learning**

- Likes stories with lots of action.
- Needs to move, touch, and feel in order to process information.
- The *"entertainer"* in class.

What are some other characteristics of the Kinesthetic TLC style? (Answers on the next page)

a. _____

b. _____

c. _____

Who does this remind you of?_____

KINESTHETIC LEARNERS: learn through moving, doing, and touching...

- They comprehend best through hands, arms, legs, and full body movement and need to be allowed to work standing and move.
- Does the "process dance." After being given directions, the kinesthetic will start to move. They'll get up to get a book and go back and sit down, get a drink of water and sit down, sharpen a pencil and sit down. Find another reason to get up and sit down. What they're actually doing is processing the "directions" of the assignment.
- Will have trouble concentrating or remembering what they read if they've been sitting for too long. Needs to learn to make "mental movies".
- Often labeled as "hyperactive, ADD, or ADHD".

So, for easier "K Style" learning:

- Take lots of breaks while studying and move around when you are learning new things. Pace while you recite and use hand gestures to remember.
- Have standing work periods.
- Toss and catch a bean bag, squish some Play-doh, or chew gum when taking in new information and while studying.
- Use bright colors to highlight reading material, color code your subjects, and decorate your study area with pictures/posters.
- Play background music while studying.
- Do the classroom activities rather than just sitting on the sidelines or reading about it in a book.
- Draw, doodle, or take notes during a lecture.
- Act out what you read, design a game, or use flash cards.
- Write things down in *"three's"* when studying for tests. Write, rewrite, condense, and abbreviate as you go.
- Connect what you learn to a movie or personal experience.
- Teach the material to someone else.

TLC TIP:
Give your child several choices of preferred (those that she really wants to do) activities to do when you are busy. This provides structure and decreases their chance of causing trouble for you.

Since K's learn by "hands-on", if we don't give them something to put their hands on, they will put their hands on something. This is how they explore and experiment with their world. Notice when you go to the store, they are the ones that you tell over and over, "Don't touch...put that back...come over here, now!"

To eliminate the problem easier, have smaller children bring an intriguing toy to play with while sitting in the basket. Send older kids on "same isle" (where you can see them) errands, picking out the item that you ask for. In some stores, they now have Jr. baskets for kids to push along and shop. Brilliant!

The key is have something to keep them occupied, so your shopping or busy time can be even more productive and enjoyable. Now who wouldn't benefit from that?

d. Easier "V Style" Learning

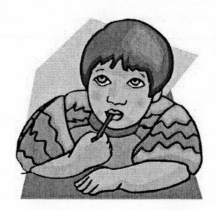

- Learns by seeing. Eyes go up.
- More quiet and organized.
- *Can* sit still for long periods of time.

What are some other characteristics of the Visual TLC style? (Answers on the next page)

a. _____

b. _____

c. _____

Who does this remind you of?_____

VISUAL LEARNERS: learn through seeing…

- These learners learn best by watching demonstrations, interpreting facial expressions and body language. They'll go astray if they can't "see".
- They like information illustrated on charts, graphs, overheads, in videos, etc.
- Can easily play a "mental movie" of what they read. Can make their inner pictures bigger, colourful, and add shape and dimensions, as well.
- Normally uses visualization to spell accurately and remember what they read.
- Learns well with descriptions and demonstrations.
- Organizes with lists.

So, for easier "V Style" learning:

- Use pictures, charts, maps and graphs to help you see the information clearly.
- Use color or *post-its* to highlight important points in your textbooks.
- Take notes or ask for handouts.
- Use graphs to organize your notes by main idea and supporting details.
- Draw pictures or images to illustrate your ideas before writing them down.
- Read illustrated books. Write and illustrate a story.
- Use multi-media (computers, videos and film).
- Study in a quiet place.
- Write things down in *"three's"* when studying for tests. Write, rewrite, condense and abbreviate.
- After reading, play a "mental movie" of what you read.
- Ask for written instructions when directions are given verbally.

Assessment One

e. Discover Your Personal TLC Style

Rank these statements in order from **greatest to least**. Put a number **3** next to the one that best describes you, a number **2** beside the one that somewhat describes you and a **1** next to the phrase that least describes you.

1. When I'm teaching someone how to do something, I usually:
   - ❑ a. show them with diagrams, posters, and drawings.
   - ❑ b. tell them how to do it.
   - ❑ c. do it for them or let them try for themselves.

2. When I'm spelling a word, I usually:
   - ❑ a. see the word in my mind's eye (visualize).
   - ❑ b. sound it out.
   - ❑ c. write it down then check whether it feels right.

3. When I come in contact with someone again, it's easier for me to remember:
   - ❑ a. their face.
   - ❑ b. their name.
   - ❑ c. what we did when we were together.

4. I can read someone's mood by:
   - ❑ a. the look on their face.
   - ❑ b. the loudness, softness, or the tone of their voice.
   - ❑ c. the way they move.

5. When I'm working on an assignment, I'm easily distracted:
   - ❑ a. when things look out of place.
   - ❑ b. by noises.
   - ❑ c. when I can't finish something, or I'm unable to move.

6. When I think of my best friend, I mostly:
   - ❑ a. see what they look like, a place we went to together, or some other mental picture or image.
   - ❑ b. hear the sound of their voice.
   - ❑ c. feel some kind of an emotion (excitement, calmness, happiness, etc.).

7. When I'm feeling bored, I will usually:
   - ❑ a. draw, doodle, or watch something.
   - ❑ b. hum, drum on the table, or talk to someone.
   - ❑ c. move.

8. When watching a movie that I really enjoy, it's mostly because of:
   - ❑ a. the descriptive and colorful scenery
   - ❑ b. interesting and lively dialogue between the characters.
   - ❑ c. the action and adventure.

9. When I'm putting something together, I usually:
   - ❑ a. look at the directions and the picture.
   - ❑ b. talk with someone or find myself talking out loud as I work.
   - ❑ c. put the directions aside and figure it out as I go.

10. When I imagine myself at the beach, I mostly:
    - ❑ a. see my surroundings.
    - ❑ b. hear the seagulls and the rush of the waves.
    - ❑ c. feel the breeze on my face, sand on my feet, and the warmth of the sun.

11. When learning something new, it's easier to understand when I:
    - ❑ a. see pictures or demonstrations.
    - ❑ b. hear a lecture or talk about it.
    - ❑ c. actually practice it.

12. I am most likely to be drawn to someone:
    - ❑ a. who looks attractive or smart.
    - ❑ b. who says all the right words in the right way.
    - ❑ c. who gives me a good feeling.

14. Something is more believable when:
    - ❑ a. I can clearly see it.
    - ❑ b. it sounds credible.
    - ❑ c. it feels real.

15. When I enter a room:
    - ❑ a. I see all the bright colors and the way things look.
    - ❑ b. I hear all the voices and sounds in my surroundings.
    - ❑ c. get a feeling about what is going on.

How to Score:
Use the TLC Scoring Chart on the next page to copy the numbers you wrote in your answers. All *"a"* answers show a Visual preference, the *"b's"* suggest Auditory, and *"c's"* point to a Kinesthetic TLC style. Go back to question number 1 and

- ❑ a. **Copy** the number that you wrote in box "a" in the chart under the Visual heading.
- ❑ b. **Put** the number that you wrote in box "b" in the Auditory column.
- ❑ c. **Copy** the number that you wrote in box "c" in the Kinesthetic column.

Now do the same for each of your 15 questions and answers until each box in the chart has a number. Then add up the totals for each TLC preference (V, A, K). The higher the score, the more likely you are to use this sense as a way of thinking, learning, and communicating. There are no wrong or right answers.

TLC Scoring Chart

Visual	Auditory	Kinesthetic
1.		
2.		
3.		
4.		
5.		
6.		
7.		
8.		
9.		
10.		
11.		
12.		
13.		
14.		
Totals:		

Analyzing Your Score

1. The highest score indicates your preference. The lowest score indicates your least developed modality.
2. If your two highest scores are the same or very close, both of these modalities may be your preference.
3. If all three of your scores are identical, you have truly developed and can work equally well in any of the modalities.

We call this, "Talented and Gifted"

TLC TIP:
Have your Kinesthetic do "standing work periods". Purchase an inexpensive white board (magnetic ones are best) for him to work out his math problems on. Then you can take a picture of two or three problems to "show his work" to the teacher. Often the math worksheets are cramped with too many problems on one page and not enough room for students to work them out.

Extension:

- Get a magnetic white board and some magnetic numbers for your child to use while doing his math, so that he has the ability to manipulate and move the numbers around.
- Magnetic letters are used to arrange spelling or vocabulary words.
- Have your child use pictures (draw, or magazine cut-outs) on the white board to remember definitions.
- Your child can write her spelling words BIG using big arm movements.

4. Ten Multi-Sensory Activities for Strengthening Learning

Lower scores show that the modality *(TLC style)* may not be being used enough. Let's figure out why. One reason is that there may be a physical or neurological impairment that interrupts your child from using the modality successfully.

A more common reason is that he or she hasn't had enough experience using the modality effectively in school. Often, these students get labelled as "at risk". Therefore, it becomes necessary to help your child strengthen his or her use of all the modalities, which will automatically strengthen learning. The following activities will help you do just that:

   a.   Multi-Sensory Memory
   b.   See It and Say It
   c.   Hear It and Say It
   d.   Multi-sensory-Connect Reading Strategy
   e.   Eye-Level Reading
   f.   Reading Assignment Task Analysis
   g.   Increase Your Child's Interest in Reading Easier
   h.   Power Memory Strategies
   i.   Good Spelling Faster
   j.   The Math Connection

Is *this* learning?

The more senses you involve…the greater the learning.

Activity A

a. Multi-Sensory Memory

For each subject listed below, have your child imagine and share a sensory experience for each category.

Category:

A picture or image	A sound or voice	A touch, sensation, or emotion	A smell	A taste

Subject:

1.   The beach
2.   A restaurant you like
3.   The last movie you saw
4.   Something that makes you laugh
5.   Where you were last Saturday
6.   Your favorite toy
7.   Your favorite teacher
8.   Your best friend
9.   An amusement park
10.   A time when you felt positive, strong, and happy

Activities B and C

b. See It, Hear It...and Say It

Use the pictures on the following pages to strengthen visual and auditory TLC styles of learning and memory.

Visual Procedure: (See It...Say It)
1. Child looks at the first group of 3 pictures (row A) for up to 30 seconds.
2. Cover the pictures. Have child tell sequence of pictures.
3. Show second group of 4 pictures (row B) for up to 30 seconds.
4. Cover them and have child state from memory.
5. Continue with row C, D, etc. to find the number of items easily remembered.

Auditory Procedure: (Hear It...Say It)
Follow the same pattern as in the visual EXCEPT you will **say** the picture sequence (up to 3 times). Child does not look at them.

Note: You can use other pictures or items at home to do this activity at least once or twice a week to help increase your child's visual and auditory memory. Use the checklist on the next page to chart progress.

Sometimes students will remember all of the pictures, but recall them OUT OF SEQUENCE (sequential memory). That explains the columns entitled, *"Number of pictures correct,"* versus *"Number of pictures in sequence."* (*Variation:* Have your child "see the pictures" and then draw them. Stick figures are fine).

In order to increase your child's ability to "visualize", hold the pictures at eye level or above while they "take mental pictures" of them. Then have them **look up** in order to recall the pictures. (See *"The Eyes Tell It All"* on page 39 for a thorough explanation why).

When your child remembers all 8 pictures, add more images to stretch the memory.

Increasing Visual Memory Checklist
See it...Say it

TLC Style	Time/ repetitions (30 sec. max.)	Number of pictures remembered	Number of pictures recalled in sequence/ Comments:
Visual			
Visual			
Visual			

Increasing Auditory Memory Checklist
Hear it...Say It

TLC Style	Time/ repetitions (3 repetitions)	Number of pictures remembered	Number of pictures recalled in sequence/ Comments:
Auditory			
Auditory			
Auditory			

b. See It…Say It

A.

B.

C.

D.

E.

F.

c. Hear It… Say It

A.

(Example) Say: *glasses, football, pencil*

B.

C.

D.

E.

F.

A Reading Success Story (and how we did it)

A few years ago, I was asked to help a sixth grade boy who's reading comprehension was between a first and second grade level. After talking with him for a few minutes, I discovered that Brian really was able and bright, but had not been operating up to his capabilities.

I suspected that Brian had never learned how to read **visually**. I asked him to read a passage from a sixth-grade level reader. I discovered several behaviors that interfered with his comprehension.

First, I noticed that when he read, he held the book, so that his eyes looked down on the page. Also, if he didn't recognize a word, he'd try to "sound it out". He didn't read fluently, with expression, but in a consistent, monotone, one word at a time. When I ask him what happened in the story, he literally repeats words that are on the page, rather than saying what the story is about.

I ask him what is going on in his head while he is reading. He states that as soon as he starts to read, his inner voice takes over. All kinds of thoughts flood his mind. He starts thinking about something he'd heard on TV, his mother's voice, or events he'd planned to do, etc. So, that by the time he read the end of a paragraph, he had no idea of what he had read.

Brian was using the sounding out strategy. People who use this technique become stuck because for them reading means saying all the words to themselves. They mistakenly believe that you can only get meaning by saying the word. They confuse comprehension with pronunciation, when often sounding out gets in the way. So, we use flash cards to train him how to respond automatically to words.

We also have him hold the book slightly above eye level. Instantly, his reading became smoother, with emphasis and tonal inflections. It's also easier to form mental images when the book is higher because when your eyes are looking up, it puts the brain in *"see"* mode.

Finally, we have him read one sentence at a time, look up, and make a mental movie of what he reads *(Multi-Sensory Reading Connect Strategy)*. His mother continues this process at home. After several weeks, Brian's reading comprehension jumps two grade levels. The follow up showed that these new strategies were producing the desired results, and last time I heard, Brian had no more reading problems.

For the  of It

Read the following and allow your mind to work out a meaning that fits for you in the time and in the way that is right for you.

I cdnuolt blveiee taht I cluod auctluly uesdnatnrd waht I was rdgnieg. The phaonmneel pweor of the hmuan mnid. Aoccdrnig to a rscheearcr at Cmagbride Uinervtisy, it deosn't mttaer in waht oredr the ltteers of a wrod are, the olny iprmoatnt tihng is taht the frist and lsat ltteer be in the rghit pclae. The rset can be a taotl mses and you can sitll raed it wouthit a porbelm.

Tihs is bcuseae the huamn mnid deos not raed ervey lteter by istlef, but the wrod as a wlohe. Amzanig huh?

Yaeh and I awlyas thought slpelng and knwng wht the wrd is was ipmorantt!

—from an email message

---

1. What did you discover?

   _____

2. What does this show you about your child having to recognize every word?

   _____

3. How will you apply what you discovered so that your child reads faster and easier?

   _____

Do it now! And you'll get to really understand…

The Eyes Tell It All

Someone once said, "The eyes are the mirror to the soul." Well, I don't know just how much of someone's soul you can see, but I do know that by watching someone's eye movements, and seeing whether they go left, right, up, or down, you can gain tremendous insight into the TLC style that they are operating in at that moment. People will be amazed at your ability to read *how* their mind is working.

The position of the eyes is a most powerful indicator of how a person is processing information. Did you know that just having students "look up" helps them in subjects like, spelling, reading comprehension, and memorization?

It is no surprise that good spellers "see" the word in their mind's eye. Those who have trouble with spelling are usually trying to sound the word out, or spell *phonetically*. But, that doesn't work. You can't even spell phonetically, phonetically.

In addition, Visuals usually see movies in their heads of what they read. This is where the comprehension is—in the pictures. Auditories and Kinesthetics who don't know how to visualize what they read will most likely have trouble answering comprehension questions. Often, they read a page and then realize that they don't know what they've just read. This can be corrected simply by shifting the position of the eyes. (*See the chart on the next page.)

That Inner Voice

You ever sit down to read and as soon as you start, all kinds of thoughts start flowing through your head? That means you're talking to yourself. Most likely your eyes are down-left, (since you're probably holding the book down). And you know how hard it is to concentrate on what you read when you're thinking about the bills, the unfinished project at work, or the conversation you had with...

So, eliminate this problem by holding the book slightly above eye level. This shuts that inner voice off and turns on your capacity for creating mental movies. Ah, and that my friend is where the comprehension is.

*The following chart describes normally oriented right-handed people. If you are left-handed, it's reversed. A small percentage of people don't fit into this mold, but they do have their own consistent pattern.

Eye Positions and TLC

In the visual memory.

In the imagination.

Recalling what you've
heard before.

Putting words together for
speaking.

Talking to yourself.

Feeling emotion or physical
sensation.

Activity D

d. Multi-Sensory-Connect Reading Strategy

When reading, some students are so busy trying to figure out the words that they don't get the whole picture of what they are reading. Students who don't see the whole picture of what they read usually have trouble with comprehension. A powerful strategy to help your child increase his or her comprehension is the multi-sensory reading technique. Simply put, you help your child connect what (s)he's reading to the five senses. Here's how to do it.

A. Read a book to your child that is slightly higher than his or her reading level. Have child look up and see a mental movie of what you read. Since comprehension is in the pictures, it is important to have him/her describe in detail what (s)he sees.

1. Ask *sensory* questions about what you read every one-three sentences.

   - What do you see?
   - What do you hear?
   - What textures might the character be touching?
   - How does this character feel?
   - Are there any smells and tastes associated with this section of the story? If so, what are they?

2. Ask *connection* questions every paragraph or two.

   1. Compare this story to a movie, color, or song, etc.
   2. What does this story show you about life?
      - relationships?
   3. Give an example of_____.
   4. Put it in your own words.
   5. What's your opinion about_____?
   6. Apply this to a past experience.

Have your child use the (5W + H) strategy: Who, What, When, Where, Why, and How. Asking these questions focuses the mind, making you better prepared to comprehend easier.

TLC TIP:
Allow your child to choose the best reading position that matches the goal or results (comfort, memory, comprehension, etc.).

It's interesting that people easily "get" what happened in the story when they lay down to read a good book. Then, they sit at a desk and have problems getting the main idea of a History reading assignment. Often, when you're reading academic information, doing whatever it takes to stay calm, relaxed, and comfortable is necessary to taking in, comprehending, and remembering the information.

Reading while standing or pacing often stimulates a "lethargic" mind. It will shake them out of that mental nap, especially if they link what they read with a memory. The more rich and pleasant associations they are able to draw upon, the more they will read and the better retention and they will to have.

Sitting can be used to achieve your goals as well. What can your child best accomplish in this position? Increasing speed? Organizing information?

When you're sitting, can you tune in to what you're reading so much, that the rest rest of the world quiets and seems to move in slow motion? If not, what position will allow you to do that?

Have your child try them and discover which body position increases his or her excitement level, motivation, or relaxes and opens his or her mind to external information. You'll both be amazed at the results.

Activity E

e. Eye-Level Reading
Creating Mental Movies

Try this little experiment.

Have your child place the book on the table and read aloud. His eyes will be looking down as he reads to you. You will notice that his reading is slower and less fluent.

Next, have him raise the book slightly above eye level. Having him place his elbows on the table and cradling the book in his hands can do this. You will instantly hear that his reading becomes faster and even more fluent. Why is this so?

When the eyes are down, the student may be talking to himself, trying to "figure" out the words, and so loses overall meaning of the text.

So, the ***process*** for eye-level reading is;

1. Student holds the book at eye level or slightly above. He reads several sentences.
2. Ask **sensory-questions**. Have student describe in detail (color, size, texture, type, etc.), what he or she sees.
3. Ask **connection-questions**. Have student connect the information to his or her own experience.

TLC TIP:
*Have your child draw a picture or a diagram that represents what she is reading. It doesn't have to make sense to anyone but her. If she's reading about people, draw stick figures. Or, she could draw a figure, seeing a "mental movie", to show what's important on this page.

f. Reading Assignment Task Analysis

In school, your child has *multiple reading assignments*. Students who can figure out what to do with the information get better grades easier.

Here's a way to do it.
1. Have your child check the assignment. Most reading assignments fall into one of the following categories.

___Read and participate in class discussion
___Read and take notes
___Read and tell others about it
___Read and apply the information
___Read and remember for quiz/test
___Read and write a review and/or reaction
___Read and answer questions

2. Post the following list on the next page and have him or her tell you which task is assigned.

Activity F

Reading Assignment Task Analysis

What do you need to do with this reading assignment?

___Read and participate in class discussion
___Read and take notes
___Read and tell others about it
___Read and apply the information
___Read and remember for quiz/test
___Read and write a review and/or reaction
___Read and answer questions*

*TLC TIP (VAK)
Review questions BEFORE reading each section. You'll find answers faster and easier.

Activity G

g. **Increase Your Child's Interest In Reading Easier**

Use the newspaper or magazine to help your child develop an interest for reading and love for learning. You will inadvertently build your child's interest in reading. That will automatically increase the amount of time that he or she reads. The more they read, the better readers they become. Better reading=better grades.

Just have them do this activity at least once a week and share the results with you. It takes about 15-20 minutes. (Use this time to get in a little reading enjoyment for yourself and you make it even more effective). Mornings usually work best BEFORE they get sucked into the tube.

1. Make copies of the activity sheet on the following page, or just have your child draw and label the columns on a separate sheet of paper.
2. Have your child read and follow the directions accurately.
3. Enjoy listening to your child briefly share it with you!

Variation:
During trips in the car, your child can read short selections. Then you can ask him or her the questions.

I Feel Very Curious About...

Directions: Grab a sheet of paper and pencil. Copy the chart below big enough for you to have room to write your answers. Pick an article from a newspaper or magazine that interests you. Then, as you read the article:

1. List each new *subject* (who or what they're talking about) you run into in a word or phrase.
2. Check the column to show whether you *liked* or *disliked* what you read.
3. Ask any question about the subject.
4. List something you discovered.

Your paper might look something like this but with bigger boxes.

Subject:	Liked:	Disliked:	Questions:	Discovered:

TLC TIP
Help you child create a purpose for reading. It will get him through the assignment faster and he will know exactly what to expect.

A. Before reading any book, suggest to your child "look at the title and ask yourself the following questions":

1. *What is this book about?*
2. *What do I already know about the subject?*
3. *What do I want to discover about this subject?*
4. *What do I want to get out of reading this book?*

B. Read the index or the table of contents.

Your child will be astounded at how much he already knows when he starts the reading assignment. He's already got a heads up on the information and his mind will be geared toward recognizing main ideas and key points. This skill is crucial to your child's success in school.

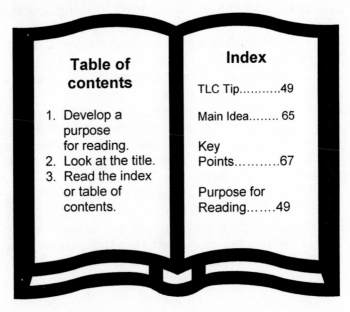

Table of contents

1. Develop a purpose for reading.
2. Look at the title.
3. Read the index or table of contents.

Index

Ten EZR Ways to Increase Reading Comprehension

1.   Read to your children, even the older ones. It's never too early or too late to start. The popularity of books on CD shows we never stop enjoying being read to.
(For older kids, just tell them something like, *"I have to practice reading to an audience. Thanks for indulging me. Oh, and feel free to let me know what I can do to make it even better"*

2.   Use the Multi-Sensory-Connect Reading Strategy.

3.   Teach your child to Eye-Level Read.

4.   Tell a humorous story from your childhood and have your child illustrate it.

5.   Connect a new concept to something your child already gets. "It's like a train but it has..."

6.   Cut out the headings and the articles on a page of the newspaper. Have your child reassemble the page placing the correct article with each title. As the child gets more advanced, cut the page into groups of several or even single paragraphs to reassemble. Hmmm, interesting!

7.   When there are questions to answer, have your child review the questions BEFORE reading the material.

8.   Take favorite books or books on CD when traveling in the car.

9.   Model reading enjoyment. Read magazines, newspapers, and books in the presence of your child.

10.   Use the reading assignment task analysis.

TLC TIP
- Have your child read the questions at the end of an assignment BEFORE reading so he or she will recognize the answers when he or she gets to them.
- Use a Post-it to mark the paragraph in which the answer is found to one of the questions.

h. Power Memory Strategies

Train your child to:
a. Do whatever it takes to get it right the first time.
- Read, read, and read some more.
- Ask questions and get help.
- Put it in your own words.

b. Connect it to the senses.
- Picture it in your mind's eye and draw it.
- Hear the sounds associated with it.
- Compare it to a movie, story, or real life experience.

c. Sort and organize the information.
- Make up your own filing system.
- Use chapter titles, sub-titles, tables, graphs, flowcharts, and diagrams to find what's important.
- Create possible test questions using sample problems as a guide.

TLC-Tip:
Use different areas and colors on a wall, in a room, or in a house, etc., to categorize information.

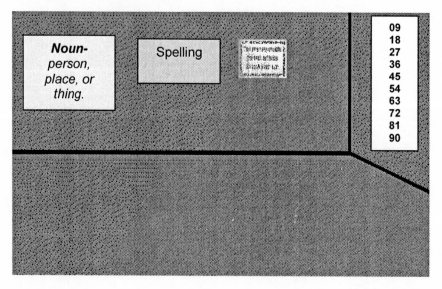

Activity H

Memorize Without Working Hard

Often, your child has something he or she needs to remember such as, spelling or vocabulary words, multiplication tables, or even a list of chores, you can help them remember faster and easier by using ceiling notes.

How to use wall or ceiling notes
1. Get 5"X8" index cards.
2. Have them write the information **briefly**, legibly, and large enough in their favorite color. Outline in black for visibility if needed. They can type the info as well.
3. Post it on a wall or the ceiling using tape, poster putty (for hanging posters) usually comes right off and can be used over and over.

Wall/Ceiling Notes (Examples)

Motivational

I do whatever it takes to
get the good grades I
deserve.

Multiplication tables

09
18
27
36
45
54
63
72
81
90
99
108

Grammar rules

Noun

Names a person,
place, or thing.
(car, book, or $)

Spelling/Vocabulary

regulate

53

TLC-Tip:
Post the nine-times-tables on the ceiling, or high on the wall. Have your child look at, recite while pacing, or jumping on a mini trampoline, information to be remembered.

Variation: Use music and movement while reciting. This technique can be used for any kind of memory work. (P.S. Remind him to *tie his shoes*).

Make your TLC style work for you:
- Move around when you are learning new things.
- Pace and recite to remember.
- Listen to background music while studying.

Activity I

i. Good Spelling Faster

1. One trick when posting spelling words is to capitalize any smaller words that are inside the bigger word.

occuPIEd

2. Another powerful strategy is to break larger words down into smaller, visually stimulating chunks.

sim ul TAN eo US

3. Have your child illustrate the word by drawing, or cutting and pasting a magazine picture to the word.

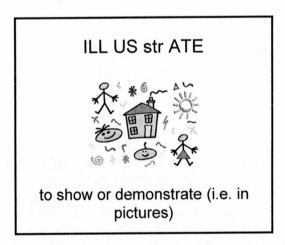

ILL US str ATE

to show or demonstrate (i.e. in pictures)

Good spelling is as easy as one, two, three!

Activity J

j. The Math Connection

Help Them "Get it" by Recognizing Patterns

One sure way to do this is to have them connect the concept with something that they already know, help them to recognize patterns, an teach them how to utilize their visual memory and you've unleashed a powerful formula for making the process of learning easier, which will automatically make it more enjoyable for you. Look at the following example:

Patterns in Multiplication Tables

Below is a listing of the nine-times-tables. The answers are broken down into columns. Look closely.

		Column One	Column Two
9 X 1 =	09	0	9
9 X 2 =	18	1	8
9 X 3 =	27	2	7
9 X 4 =	36	3	6
9 X 5 =	45	4	5
9 X 6 =	54	5	4
9 X 7 =	63	6	3
9 X 8 =	72	7	2
9 X 9 =	81	8	1
9 X 10 =	90	9	0

Read the numbers in column one going down. Now read the numbers in column two the same way. Did you catch it? You've probably figured out that the answers are the same as counting. The first column going down goes like this: "0,1,2,3,4,5,6,7,8,9." While the second column going down reads; "9,8,7,6,5,4,3,2,1,0." BRILLIANT!

Do you see any other patterns? How are the numbers in column one different than the numbers in column two? How are they the same?

*09,18,27,36,45,**54,63,72,81,90***

Do you notice that the answers go so far and then switch? Same numbers, different order. FASCINATING! How about if I ask you to take each answer and make up an addition problem. That is, add the number in column one to the number in column two.

0+9=__, 1+8=__, 2+7=__, 3+6=__, 4+5=__, 5+4=__ and so on...

You see it! The answers are all the same, "9." Yes, patterns make it easier. You're probably wondering if there is a pattern for the other times tables. What do you think? Try it with the "eights." Set the answers up in columns and study them carefully.

8 x 1 = _____   _____
8 x 2 = _____   _____
8 x 3 = _____   _____
8 x 4 = _____   _____
8 x 5 = _____   _____
8 x 6 = _____   _____
8 x 7 = _____   _____
8 x 8 = _____   _____
8 x 9 = _____   _____
8 x 10 =_____   _____

Remember, there are *unlimited possibilities* for finding the *right solution.*

TLC-Tip:
Use Multi-Sensory Memorization to help your child remember facts and important information for tests.

1. Post the information to be memorized on the wall (upper left if your child is right-handed, or place it so they are looking up and to the right if they are left-handed).
2. Have your child jump on a mini-trampoline as she recites, and looks at posted (on the wall) info to be remembered.
3. Test them by having them look away from the posted information and recite from memory. Remind them to *look up and see it* in their mind's eye.

   Kinesthetics move a lot. They will do it whether we want them to or not. Might as well put it to good use. This way, everybody benefits. Huh? Yes.

TLC TIP:
Have your child color code each subject in his/her notebook. Use multi-colored dividers. For example, math can be blue, English-green, history-brown, etc.

- Also, use a separate folder for homework.
- Completed, to be turned in on the right.
- Work to be completed on the left.

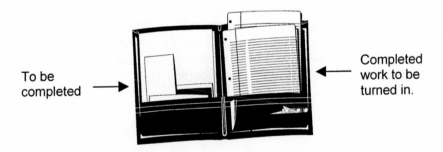

To be completed → ← Completed work to be turned in.

5. Getting Kids To Say YES When They Want To Say NO

"Don't you ever listen?" Mr. Jones frowned at his son. Despite the fact that he'd told David to take out the trash, put his laundry in the proper place, and complete his homework, everyday for the last six months it seemed, things still were not getting done. And now, here David was sitting in front of the TV again...

Most of us can identify with this. We give our kids directions, we tell them what we want them to do but it seems that no matter what we say, someone always doesn't seem to know exactly what to do. Why is that?

Here are several possible reasons. Often, the verbal directions we give our kids are multiple in nature. We tell them to do several things at once and of course, since they usually only exercise their selective memory when it comes to things like chores and school work, they tend to conveniently forget some parts, if not everything we've said.

So, having a visual (non-verbal) to go along with what we say (verbal), we **double the length of their memory,** and students don't have to depend on us for the information, they can **see it for themselves.**

You will find in this section some powerful strategies to use with your child or for yourself. They are designed **to motivate, inspire, and empower** the participant. Is this something that you want for you and your child? Imagine what you all can accomplish.

Strategy One

Laminated Visuals

Here are a few samples of Laminated Visuals (laminated ready made sheets with all the necessary information). They are easy to use over and over.

- Use a *wipe-off* marker to check all the areas you want your child to complete at any given time.
- If they have any questions, write the answers on the laminate as well.
- Saves lots of time and your voice too.

Sample:

Rules

1. Get your homework done BEFORE watching TV, playing video games, or other recreational activities.

2. Phone times _____am/pm to_____am/pm. (provided homework is done).

3. Chores completed by_____am/pm.

Sample

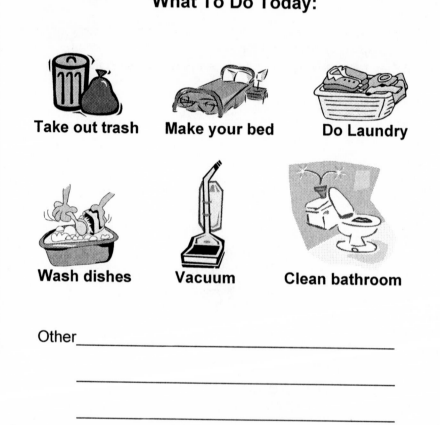

What To Do Today:

Take out trash   **Make your bed**   **Do Laundry**

Wash dishes   **Vacuum**   **Clean bathroom**

Other_____

_____

_____

The more information you have written down, the more visual you get, the less your child has to depend on you. They will learn to take responsibility for their own behavior. Now who *doesn't* want that?

Or, you *could* handle it this way?

If you decide to scream, yell, or tell them over and over, will that work without causing any more pressure, difficulties, or stress for you? If it doesn't work, does it make sense to continue something that is not working? No. Therefore, because of your new understanding, in the future, you will become aware that you are automatically using the techniques you've discovered in this book with your child(ren). So, that they will surprise you and themselves with how easily and how well they cooperate, leaving you deeply satisfied.

Strategy Two

"Point" Notes

In the business world, there is often so much information to pass on to so many people that it becomes necessary to write it down. It is a time saver. It also helps people understand exactly what is required.

"POINT" NOTES

When dealing with problems or giving negative information to your child, you can use the same principle. Put the information on a piece of paper. Having a piece of paper, or (if paper's not available), some other inanimate object, or some point off in space, (to represent the problem) to *"point"* to and look at when talking about the problem, means your child won't internalize himself as being the problem.   Instead, it is the paper that becomes the "bad guy". It's faster and far easier to get to the solution. (Sample "Point Notes" on the following page.)

Stress-less Discipline
- Use a sheet of paper to point to when you're talking about the problem.
- When your child talks, it's ok to look at them and nod.
- However, when it's your turn to speak, point to and refer back to the info on the sheet.

Try it for yourself and you can decide how best to use it to accomplish exactly what you want to accomplish. And you'll avoid a whole lot of needless problems, too.

Sample

"Point" Notes

Discussion with:_____ Date_____

Issue/Situation:

_____

_____

Need to Know Info:

_____

_____

Expectations: (Make sure that they are behavior specific):

_____

_____

Necessary Follow-up:

_____

_____

Our Agreements:

_____

_____

Other Important Information:

_____

_____

TLC Tip
When disciplining or correcting your child, sit or stand strategically.

Often, as caring parents, we find ourselves having to discipline our kids. Sometimes we (or they) come in already feeling frustrated, overworked, and just simply, "tired" of having to deal with the everyday issues of life. We may have to give them some unpleasant information. If we're not careful, they could unleash these pent-up emotions on us.

One way to dramatically lessen that possibility is to sit (or stand) strategically. Sit in such as way as to suggest to them that you are not *blaming* them. You really are *"on their side"* and want to find a solution. Often, this positioning along with the "point note" strategy makes the difference.

When giving your child positive information:	When giving negative information or consequences:

1. Sitting at **opposite** positions is ok. 2. Using **eye-to-eye** communication is fine. 3. Praise their **effort**	1. Position yourself **perpendicular** to person. 2. Use "point notes" **(eye-to-task)** to look at or refer to when talking about problem. 3. They'll perceive you as being **on "their" side**.

When was the last time you met with your child(ren), discussed the pertinent information, found a solution, and got out of there feeling positive, strong, and happy? Well, if this is what you really want, consider these powerful techniques and just go do it!

Strategy Three

WAKE UP TIME MADE EASIER

Ever tried to wake one of these? (Especially when you're running late). A child who takes too long (in our opinion) to wake up can be the cause of much stress. What if you discovered a way to get them up faster and easier? Well, try this.

About fifteen minutes BEFORE you want him up, go into the room and say, "Johnny, in fifteen minutes you will wake up." Then leave. Don't worry that he's sleeping, his inner mind will hear you. Ten minutes later, go back into the room and say, "Johnny, in five minutes you will get up and get ready for school." Again leave. Five minutes later, return and say, "Johnny, time to get up now and get ready for school." (That is if he isn't already up). IF he's already up, **praise his *effort*.** You can say something like, "It took tremendous *effort* for you to get up on your own. I appreciate it."

Why does this work? Well, anytime someone is doing something that they enjoy, that means that they are in their *"pleasure principle"*. Asking them to do something that will interrupt their pleasure will usually get you some type of resistance. Whether it's whining, complaining, ignoring, or simply refusing, etc.

In order to get someone out of their pleasure principle and into their *computer mode* (problem solving or work mode) you need to give them *time*. They unconsciously use this time to *prepare* themselves for the task ahead. When you give them the necessary time, they perceive you as being fair. *That* alone can eliminate disastrous results.

It's kind of like the traffic signal concept. Back in the day, there were only red and green lights. Why do you suppose they added the yellow light? Yes. Since the lights went straight from green to red, there was no *preparation* time and too many collisions. The yellow light let drivers know what's coming next. It has prevented many crashes.

List three additional times you could use this strategy:

1._____

2._____

3._____

Strategy Four

Ten Enjoyable Steps to a Successful Day

You and your child find a quiet, relaxing spot where you can complete this exercise right before going to sleep when needed.

In a calm voice, say:
Close your eyes and listen deeply. Picture yourself having a successful day in school.

1. See yourself sitting at your desk, reading, writing, and accurately completing *all* of your assignments. What are you doing?
2. Watch yourself appropriately getting any help that you may need from the teacher. What are you doing?
3. See how skilled you are at avoiding any potential problems. How did you do it?
4. Listen to your successful self-talk. What are you saying to yourself?
5. Feel now how good it feels to encourage yourself. How does it feel?
6. Watch yourself behave intelligently in a way that satisfies all the needs of your total personality. What are you doing?
7. Discover how your status is increased because of your mature behavior.
8. See yourself getting the respect that you deserve from your teacher and your peers. What are they doing?
9. Experience the feelings of success. Bask in it.
10. Consider now, how important your educational success is to you and just go do it!

When I count to three, you can open your eyes, whenever you're ready, knowing that your life is a success. One...two...three.

TLC TIP:
Use the chart on the next page and discuss with your child what a response-able student looks, sounds, and behaves like.

Have you ever asked your child how she's doing in school and she responds that she's doing fine. Then the report card comes and says something totally different.

Often, students don't do well in school because they don't know what's expected of them. The rules may be unclear. The standard operating procedure of the class may be unspecified.

Also, since there are multiple indicators that affect a student's ability to learn, it is necessary to make certain that your child "gets a grasp" on how teachers look at things.

1. First, go over the chart on the next page with your child.
2. Then, have your child ask his or her teacher what (s)he needs to do to get an "A". (They can use the form, *Ask the Teacher* in chapter eight, Additional Assessments and Resources.)
3. Finally, have your child tell you what is expected of him or her in each class.

Response-*able* Student Behavior

Uses academic time for completing assignments	Response-*able* behavior (It works for your overall success)	Contributes to effective instruction time	Effective and consistent class participation
Accurately completes and turns in all work on time.	Cooperates with the rules.	Offers helpful insights or comments.	Asks relevant questions.
Brings supplies each class period.	Rarely misses school, arrives on time.	Listens when the teacher, or others talk. Avoids interrupting.	Comments show evidence of thorough reading.
Reads and follows directions accurately.	Allows others to finish their work before engaging them in non-academic conversation.	Sticks with challenging assignments until mastered.	Allows others to express ideas or opinions without negative feedback.

Doing the things on this chart will help you achieve exactly what you want to achieve faster, easier, and more enjoyably. Choose consciously and subconsciously to get the very top grades. Then, you'll get to experience success in the time and way of your choice.

Strategy Five

Useful Life Lessons

Use these important life lessons to make a weekly motivational sign to place on the walls, ceiling, mirror, refrigerator, etc. In fact, have your child make the sign, with graphics or pictures on the computer, or cut-outs from magazines.

1. Tell the truth no matter what.
2. Learn from your experience.
3. Mistakes are costly.
4. Whatever you put out there, will come back to you.
5. For every choice there is a consequence.
6. It is better to be alone than with bad company.
7. Putting things off will make even more work for you. Is that what you really want?
8. Go to school every day, do your work, and stay out of trouble.
9. If someone trusts you, handle that trust with care.
10. People who don't know what they want usually end up getting what others think they should have.
11. When you love someone, you do what is in their best interest.
12. Cooperate with the rules or lose privileges.
13. Preserve your freedom or lose it.
14. Some people can't be trusted.
15. A friend wants to see you achieve success.
16. The past doesn't determine the present or the future. No matter what happened in the past, you do what it takes to make your future better.
17. If the teacher does something that I don't like, I will respond in ways that are respectful to myself and others.
18. Fighting in school creates even more problems.
19. I can choose to do whatever I want, but at what cost?
20. In this world, you have to give in order to get. People who don't learn this will have to deal with either the law or the mental ward.

TLC TIP:
Increase Your Child's Sense of Power

Sometimes we want our kids to accomplish certain tasks, but, they have other ideas.

Kids who don't believe that they are competent and capable will not take challenges, risks, or even make an effort. Those who see themselves as failures are unwilling to try something new because they are afraid of failing again. To achieve success and live up to their potential, kids need a sense of power; a feeling of being in control of their destiny.

When young people are encouraged to give their opinion about what goes on in their lives, they get the message that what they think is valued and important. Kids who are given choices and allowed to face the consequences of their choices, learn from their mistakes and develop effective decision-making skills. A sense of personal power increases.

Success requires effort. In order to succeed, your child must at least put forth the effort. Often, it is the amount of effort that makes the gain. Kids are more likely to make the effort when they've been involved in the decision-making, and get something *they* want out of doing it. So, in order to help your child reach success easier:

    1.   Praise his or her efforts.
    2.   Give him or her choices on a daily basis.
    3.   Use strategies six and seven.

We live in a world where you have to *give in order to get*. Kids who don't learn this at home, often become juvenile delinquents. You **give** your boss what he or she wants, you **get** your paycheck. You **give** money to **get** food, clothing, and housing. **Give** it some thought, and you will **get** the point.

Often, as well-meaning parents, we want to give our children what we didn't have. This is understandable. We want our kids to experience the good side of life. We want them to avoid the problems, trouble, and hardships that we may have gone through. So, we give them name brand clothes, shoes, playthings, etc., simply because...

The truth is, there is nothing wrong with wanting our kids to get the best in life. However, what happens when kids get whatever they want, without having to give anything in return? What message do they get about the world?

Right; that you can get something for nothing, stuff is free, and they don't have to contribute. They learn to take without giving. This is not the way of the world. This way of thinking and doing can cause them and you a whole lot of unnecessary trouble.

People who take, take, take without giving, end up in prison. On the flip side, people who give, give, give without receiving, end up in the mental ward. There has to be a balance of give and take. This is the way of the world. It's the way to success faster, easier, and more enjoyably. Show your child the way. You'll be glad you did.

Strategy Six is an effective way to find out what your child wants. Then you just tell him what he or she has to **give** in order to **get** it.

Consider and do this now. Then, you get to experience the joy of you and your child's success anyway you choose.

Strategy Six

EMPOWERING YOURSELF

You and your child get a piece of paper and pencil. Answer the following seven questions and increase your choices of getting even more of what you want easier.

1. What do I want that's important to me?

    _____

2. What's preventing me from getting that now?

    _____

3. Am I willing to pay the price?

    _____

4. What changes am I willing to make that will enhance my life?

    _____

5. What am I willing to do to effect those changes?

    _____

6. How would others know when the change has been made?

    _____

Strategy Seven

If...Then (Choices and Consequences)

Directions: You and your child can use the information on the following page to find the possible consequence that matches each choice below. Put the matching letter in the space. Briefly discuss each one with your child as you go.

IF:	THEN:

1. You entertain, clown around, or make other students laugh while the teacher is teaching...   *J*

2. You get *kicked out* of class...   _____

3. You don't *keep up* in your school assignments...   _____

4. You bring *"street behavior"* into school (i.e., stealing, cussing, fighting, etc.)...   _____

5. You do things to get the teacher to like having you in class...   _____

6. You want to have the *"good life"* you deserve...   _____

7. You don't understand how to do something...   _____

8. You don't learn from, or use your mistakes for future advantage...   _____

9. You clearly see the value of a good education...   _____

10. You believe that you can change the future by making good choices now...   _____

Possible Consequences

A. You realize that it is the key to getting out of, and staying out of poverty (being poor). A good education gives you an economic edge.

B. You find the important information that will clarify it for you so that you can take charge right away.

C. You consider and do whatever it takes to get the success you desire.

D. You'll get more privileges, more freedom, and get good grades without having to work any harder.

E. You will *miss valuable instruction*, fall behind, and may have to deal with disappointed or angry adults.

F. You may "flunk", end up working longer and harder to catch up, and create unnecessary pressure and stress for yourself.

G. That kind of behavior makes people feel unsafe. It may also convince the teacher, principal, and other adults that you need to be locked up.

H. Since mistakes can be costly, you could end up paying with not only money, but with your pride, reputation, respect, time, health, and even your life.

I. You now see clearly that the past doesn't determine the present or the future. No matter what the past, you make the choices that make the present and the future better.

J. Other students may not pay attention to the teacher. This makes it harder for her to do her job. Either the behavior leaves, or you do.

If...Then... Answers

IF:	THEN:
1. You entertain, clown around, or make other students laugh while the teacher is teaching...	J
2. You get *kicked out* of class...	E
3. You don't *keep up* in your school assignments...	F
4. You bring *"street behavior"* into school (i.e., stealing, cussing, fighting, etc.)...	G
5. You do things to get the teacher to like having you in class...	D
6. You want to have the *"good life"* you deserve...	C
7. You don't understand how to do something...	B
8. You don't learn from, or use your mistakes for future advantage...	H
9. You clearly see the value of a good education...	A
10. You believe that you can change the future by making good choices now...	I

6. Rapid Solutions To "People" Problems

This section is for parents who want to pinpoint and eliminate the barriers to your child's success and well-being. It is taken from *Straight Up! Every Teen's Guide to Success* and is designed to help you assist your child in dealing with difficult people and situations even more effectively while resisting the temptation of their peers.

It is no secret that we are dealing with more and more serious issues when it comes to our young people. Violence, poor academic performance, and other behavior problems are just some of the challenges we face. Couple this the fact that we now have the most diverse school population than we've ever had, and it now becomes necessary for your child to find more effective ways to deal with a wide range of students and teachers in ways that help them achieve success faster and easier.

Use the *ten-minute* strategies with your child to help him or her improve relationships of all sorts at home and at school. That means you can enjoy more of your time without added unnecessary stress and pressure. Is this something that you want? I thought so. So, here it is...

Directions:
1. Make copies of and have your child fill out the sheets.
2. Discuss the questions and answers (ten minutes tops).
3. Expect the best from your child, tell him so, and praise his efforts.

79

a. What to Do When the Teacher Yells At You

Answer the questions. (I'm looking for your answers, not the right answers.)

1. The teacher yells at you in front of the whole class. What's the first thing you say to yourself?

_____

(Some possible answers are, *"She's disrespecting me, This is embarrassing, Everybody's gonna think I'm weak if I don't say something back...."*)

2. What emotion (anger, fear, or ?) do you feel when the teacher yells at you?

_____

3. How do you *usually* respond if the teacher yells at you?

_____

4. When you're responding that way (in #3), what are you trying to accomplish?

_____

5. Does it work without causing you even more problems?

_____yes   _____no

Well, I want you to be curious about something. Has the thought occurred to you that if you refuse to do your work, yell, cuss, etc., when the teacher does something that you don't like, who is really getting punished?

I understand that this teacher may have stepped out of line when he or she yelled at you. I also see how you might feel like getting back at him or her. And I don't blame you for feeling that way. However, get this. If you *don't* do your work. Who suffers? Yep. You. If you yell back at her, then who gets the hammer? Uh huh, right again...YOU. If you unleash your fury on that teacher, who is going to pay the biggest price?

The truth is, when the teacher or any other adult does something that you don't like, you can respond any way you choose. You can yell, cuss, and refuse to follow directions or do your work. But, at what cost?

6. What are some of the possible consequences?

   - You get sent to the office.
   - You miss valuable instruction and fall behind in your assignments.
   - Your parents get called.
   - You get to spend some extra time in school (detention, Saturday school, etc.).

7. List several other possible effects of yelling, cussing, or refusing to do your work:

   a. _____

   b. _____

8. Now what might it *cost* you? (Check all that apply)

   _____time   _____respect

   _____money   _____good grades

   _____reputation   _____privileges

9. What else could it cost you?

   a. _____

   b. _____

Straight up!

When an adult does or says something that you don't like, using all of the following responses:

> *I'm not doing it!*
> *I'm not going to listen to what you say.*
> *I'm not going to do my work.*
> *I'm not going to make the smart choice.*
> *I'm not going to express my anger in a respectful way.*
> *I'm not going to deal with this issue at a more appropriate time.*
> *I'm not going to let you do your job.*
> *And so on, and so on, and so on...*

are bound to get back at no one but you. YOU will be the one to pay. YOU get punished. Now, is that what you *really* want?

Listen deeply: Since you are now older than when you first started school, in the future when a teacher or another adult does something that you don't like, you will respond in ways that are respectful to yourself and to others. Name two:

a. _____

b. _____

Do it now and you get to choose when and how to enjoy your success!

b. How To Get The Teacher To Say Yes More Often

In a perfect world, all students would like all teachers and vice-versa. Realistically, we don't live in a perfect world, so:

1. How do you know when a teacher doesn't like you?

   _____

2. List three things that a teacher might do when she or he doesn't like you?

   a. _____

   b. _____

   c. _____

3. When a teacher likes you what problems do you avoid?

   _____

4. Zack is dealing with a troublesome teacher who does not like having him in class. He doesn't realize that has done some things to contribute to the problem as well. List three things that *he* may have done to get on the teacher's bad side.

   a. _____

   b. _____

   c. _____

5. What behaviors could Zack do to change the situation so that it works FOR rather than against him?

Check all that apply:

a. _____Avoid creating a disturbance while others are working.
b. _____Deal with disagreements in private.
c. _____Avoid arguing with the teacher in front of the class.
d. _____Using negotiation to get what you want.
e. _____Avoid using bully tactics (fear, intimidation) to get what you want.
f. _____Use professional language.
g. _____Breathe deeply and talk calmly.
h. _____Keep questions and comments on topic.
i. _____Avoid doing things that increase yours or other's stress level.
j. _____Turn in your completed work on time.
k. _____Avoid any speech or behavior that could make adults think that you are violent, *psychotic*, or crazy.
l. _____Avoid doing anything that could make it harder for a teacher to do her job.

6. What does Zack's situation show you about:

a. relationships?_____

_____

b. life?_____

_____

c. choices and consequences?_____

_____

7. Is it possible that Zack may *want something from this teacher* in the future? Check off one or more of the things he may want.

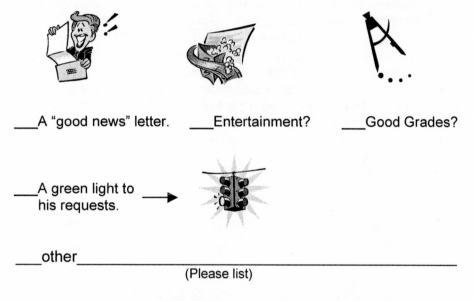

___A "good news" letter.   ___Entertainment?   ___Good Grades?

___A green light to his requests.

___other_____
                    (Please list)

During a conference with his teacher, she tells him: *When the teacher gets what she wants, it's easier to get what you want.* Zack decides to change his behavior.

Listen Deeply:
All of the reasons you had for doing things that displease your parents and teachers have now outlived their usefulness and effectiveness. You will find yourself cooperating with all helpful adults in ways that satisfy all of the needs of your total personality. And then you get to choose and enjoy the results.

Words That Win

Sometimes people say things that we don't like. They may do things that we consider rude, mean, or that violate our standards. When this happens, the temptation to take the law into your own hands and get revenge may seem sweet. When someone does something that your child doesn't like how does he or she normally respond?

If your child expresses displeasure at school, the way it's expressed in the streets, it will cause even more problems for him or her and for those closest to them. So, it becomes necessary to find ways to express strong emotion, but in a professional way.

Train your child to express emotion in ways that are respectful to himself/herself and others. Practice using the following prompts BEFORE a situation arises at home. In addition, if your child uses inappropriate language, or acts out his anger, have him/her go back and use one of the prompts on the *posted* chart to say how he/she feels and what he/she wants.

Words That Win
(Professional Language Response Chart)

When someone says or does something that you don't like, use these prompts to eliminate problems easier and get more of what you really want faster:

1. *"I feel..."*

2. *"The problem is..."*

3. *"I prefer..."*

4. *"I am aware of..."*

5. *"I want..."*

6. *"What I really mean is..."*

7. *"I am unwilling to..."*

8. *"I feel comfortable/uncomfortable with..."*

9. *"I feel displeased with..."*

10. *"I would rather..."*

11. *"Can we talk about this at another time?"*

c. Diffusing Hotheads

We all experience feelings of anger at some time or another. Discuss these concepts with your child to help him or her achieve success more enjoyably while eliminating angry outbursts. After all, don't you already have enough to deal with?

Then, consider and go over this information with your child(ren). Then, you get to choose how and when to celebrate your success.

Definitions:
   Anger (psychological explanation) = the automatic response when someone lets down your expectations, or values
   Management = what you do with anger

Issues –
   1. Whether or not a person angers easily (sign of insecurity).
   2. When they do get angry, do they handle it well? Or, is temper out-of-control?
   3. How should you behave when you're angry?

General –
   1. Anger is used in an attempt to control - ("get my way" technique).
   2. Person who is angry has not made a distinction between "*request*" and "*demand*".
      a. Request = person willingly accepts "NO".
      b. Demand = person is unwilling to accept "NO".
   3. Humans should not make demands because it means a lack of respect.

   •   **KEY - *Make requests instead of demands.***

Q & A: Where do people usually learn to use anger in an attempt to get what they want?

Parents, siblings, the media, and peers to name a few. However, the key is, any learned behavior can be unlearned and new more effective behavior can be learned.

d. What To Do With Peer Pressure

Sometimes when we're in school, our classmates try to coerce us into responding or doing something that we really don't want to do. This is known as *peer pressure.* Tell about a time when you experienced peer pressure.

_____

_____

_____

When people are trying to *force* us to do something, they will usually use one of four methods. I call these: *The Four Tools of Manipulation.* They are:

1. **Guilt** – they will say or do something to try to make us feel guilty. (*If you were really my friend, you'd...*)

2. **Fear** – this is when they say something to try and frighten us into doing what they want. *(everybody's gonna think you're weak if you don't...).*

3. **Withdrawal** – This sophisticated is often the sneakiest. They withhold their love, attention, or isolate themselves often by pretending not to hear what you said. They may ignore or give you the silent treatment.

4. **Anger** – they will use yelling, cussing, intimidation, or even bully tactics to pressure you into obeying their command.

Often, in school, the crowd will use one or more of these tactics to instigate a fight. What can you do to keep your respect and avoid unnecessary trouble? There are two things that you can do with peer pressure:
1. Resist the crowd, or
2. Lead the crowd.

Resist the crowd

Hold your left hand open, fingers together, palm facing right. Take your right fist and push, without resistance, against the palm of your left hand. Just push your left hand over as far as it will go.

Now, do the same thing except, make your left hand *resist the push*. With your left palm and right fist connected directly in front of your chest, you should feel a solidness, a balance of power, so that one arm is not working harder than the other.

This is what it is like to resist the crowd. They push one way, you simply resist their effort. Notice that your left palm didn't have to push back, it simply resisted and the fist couldn't move it. Some "resisting" phrases include:

> *I don't want to.*
> *No* (as you look extremely bored).
> *And why is that important?* (My personal favorite)
> *That doesn't fit/work for me right now.* (Another one of my favorites).

Lead the Crowd

Take your right hand and grab your left fingers. Now pull fingers to the right. Notice how easily your arm follows? It's the same when you lead the crowd. You make the first move in another direction, and they follow. Some "leading" phrases include:

> *Sounds pretty interesting, but I I'd prefer…*
> *I'd rather…*
> *I'm leaving, I'm out, let's bounce,* or whatever your favorite version of leaving is.
> *Actually, I have something more important to do.*

Saying phrases like these *while moving away from the situation*, puts you in control. Remember, when the peer pressure is on, the power really is in your hands. You can resist the crowd, or lead the crowd. This way, you'll get your respect without getting needless trouble.

So, because you are now older than when you first started school, in the future, you will become aware that you are automatically using these techniques with your peers, so that they surprise you and themselves with how easily they cooperate with helping you avoid trouble. And you'll feel deeply satisfied.

7. Conclusion

a. Everybody Loves Raymond (Another Success Story)

He was extremely kinesthetic and full of energy. He bounced around the classroom, trying to get the other kids to join in his quest for fun and adventure. He seldom completed any work. He didn't even know his ABC's. His name was written on the board, with at least 3 checks everyday! He'd missed countless recesses as he squirmed on the yellow circle and tried to tag the other kids who were happily enjoying their play time. Raymond was only in the first grade but he'd already experienced much of the failure and disappointment of not "getting it".

I met Raymond while I was working as an afternoon teacher with a group of first graders. Their regular teacher was involved in a school-wide reading program every afternoon, and so it was my job to instruct her class after they returned from lunch recess.

One of the subjects that I worked with them on was spelling. I noticed that some of the students didn't seem to be very enthusiastic about it, so I decided to try something to make it more enjoyable. I told the children that for their next spelling test, I would allow them to choose the words that they wanted to spell (oh, what did I go and do that for?).

The day finally arrived when we would construct our new spelling list. I gathered the students on the carpet, and I with marker in hand, not knowing what to expect, stood at the board. One girl raised her hand and said, "popcorn". "Hm," I thought. "I could break those two words down into, 'pop', and 'corn'". Maybe this wasn't going to be so bad after all." Two down, eight to go. A second student waved his hand frantically. I smiled bravely and called for his suggestion. "Power Ranger." He could hardly contain his excitement as the rest of the class added their "ooo's, ahhhs, and yeah's." I wrote each word separately, numbers three and four, calculating the number of letters they would have to remember for each word. "Not too bad." I was breathing a little better now.

Then someone said, "girl (four letters, ok), summer, (double letters, even better), and snow" (snow…in California? Oh well.). "Queen and galaxy" followed. Those would be fairly easy to teach since "queen" has double letters, as well as "flipsies"-letters like "n" and "u" where each flips upside down to make the other. I would also capitalize on the position of the two "a's" and the "l" in galaxy.

One more. Bodies squirmed, arms waved frantically, and voices yelled, "me, me, pick me..." as each student tried their best to get me to call on them. But, wait a minute. Who was that?

I'd been there for almost a month and this was the first time I'd seen *this* hand raised without being plunked down on someone's head. I tried not to sound too happy. "Raymond?" I called on the boy.

It seemed that as soon as the name left my lips, breathing stopped, quieted mouths hung open, and faces wore quizzical expressions, as everybody strained their necks to see just what Raymond was doing now. "Vacation!" he almost yelled loud enough for the class next door to hear. After a few seconds of shocked silence, someone countered, "Yeah, like we *need* a vacation." Everybody laughed.

Raymond had chosen the last of our ten words. He was *finally* interested enough to contribute. Now, my next challenge was, how to teach a student who didn't even know his ABC's how to spell?

Before our weekly session was over, we had drawn curves, circles, and lines that painted imaginary pictures of words. We saw the words in our mind's eye. We used our feet to trace letters on the floor. We "walked" out the letters.. Eventually, the movement cemented the letters and words into Raymond's memory, and he took his first successful spelling test ever.

Powerful suggestion:

I wanted to share this experience with you because there is something fascinating that I learned. When you allow students to learn their way, they will be more inclined to participate and they will take more responsibility for their own learning. Also, since the subject matter is stuff that they are interested in, they are automatically more motivated to learn, no matter how much of a challenge we think the work may be.

I've included a copy of Raymond's first spelling test on the next page. Check out his score. And oh, yeah...did I not mention that this boy didn't even know his ABC's? AMAZING!

Raymond's first
100% spelling test.

Samples of the
second test...WOW!

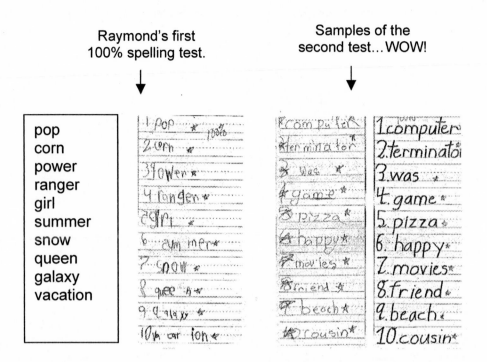

pop
corn
power
ranger
girl
summer
snow
queen
galaxy
vacation

Although Raymond's writing shows some reversals, he spelled each word correctly. He also separates the letters in a way that makes it easier for him to *"see"* them in his mind's eye (i.e., "g ala xy", and "va cat ion").

Help your child learn about his or her TLC style. Use the information in this book to help them succeed. Remember, in order to be successful in school, students are required to master lots of skills and concepts. Without effective strategies, it becomes overwhelming.

When you teach students the process of learning, they can learn any content faster, easier, and more enjoyably.

Isn't this what you really want to see: Productive, happy, and satisfied children? Imagine what could happen...

When children experience success in school, they feel better about themselves. When that happens, they are more likely to cooperate with the rules, resist the temptation of their peers, and become productive members of society. Keep your eye on the prize. And how do you help your child reach that finish line?

Because of your new understanding, in the future, you will become aware that you are automatically using the techniques and strategies you've discovered in this book with your child. So that they surprise you and themselves with how easily and how well they learn, leaving you with deep satisfaction.

8. Additional Assessments and Resources

Increase your choices of getting even more of what you really want. These additional strategies and activities are designed to assist you in helping your child experience personal and academic success easier and more enjoyably. You can decide how best to use them to accomplish exactly what you want to accomplish. And I'm positive that others will notice your efforts.

In this section, you will find:

    a. Twenty-One Suggestions for Making Learning Fun
    b. Assessment Two – Little Chunk vs. Big Chunk
    c. Three Important Questions to Ask During a Parent-Teacher-Student Conference
    d. Ask the Teacher
    e. Very Helpful Websites
    f. Other Books by this Author
    g. Contact Information

a. Twenty-One Suggestions for Making Learning Fun.

Effective Assessment Through Multiple Modalities

Visual
1. Color-code concepts.
2. Connect concept to a favorite TV show or movie.
3. Create a board game.
4. Create a picture book or magazine.
5. Create a software program.
6. Create graphs or maps.
7. Create outlines.
8. Create photo albums.
9. Decorate desks, walls, doors, or windows.
10. Design mobiles
11. Display a bulletin board.
12. Do a power point presentation.
13. Draw and explain.
14. Draw and make models.
15. Draw blueprints or building designs.
16. Illustrate situations or scenarios.
17. Make dioramas.
18. Make posters to support a position.
19. Make timelines.
20. Use pictures to show patterns or math concepts.
21. Paint.

Auditory
1. Answer exam questions out loud.
2. Compare/contrast the lesson with a favorite band, singer, or rapper and perform lyrics, poetry, or rap.
3. Connect and incorporate environmental sounds.
4. Create personal books.
5. Create a music video.
6. Debate.
7. Do regular journal writing.
8. Find and play music that relates to a topic.

9. Give an impromptu speech.
10. Paraphrase and summarize.
11. Prepare and give a lecture to classmates.
12. Prepare and give an oral report.
13. Prepare and conduct an interview.
14. Present a musical.
15. Read assigned material on tape, add sound effects.
16. Record and play a prepared speech.
17. Tell a story.
18. Use music, rhythm, or rhyme to show patterns or math concepts.
19. Write a fable, fairy tale, or other story to illustrate a concept.
20. Write essays.
21. Write lyrics to an instrumental piece.

Kinesthetic

1. Build and display model.
2. Collect materials and show how they are related to a concept.
3. Compare/contrast TV shows with concepts.
4. Conduct or lead out in a lab.
5. Connect sports to learning.
6. Create a scrapbook.
7. Create a sculpture.
8. Create and perform a dance routine.
9. Create "hands-on" learning centers.
10. Demonstrate or act out a concept.
11. Find and play a "school appropriate" movie related to a topic.
12. Integrate movement and learning.
13. Invent a game to illustrate a concept.
14. Make 3-D objects or bulletin boards.
15. Take part in the research and planning of a related field trip.
16. Teach a concept to your peers by providing a "cooperative learning" experience.
17. Team-teach a lesson/concept.
18. Use body-language or role-play.
19. Use objects to show patterns or math concepts.
20. Write and perform a play.
21. Write about how the concept relates to relationships and life.

Assessment Two

b. Little Chunk vs. Big Chunk
(Sequential or Simultaneous Learner)

Check the one that *most* describes your way of doing things:

1. When I read a book, I usually:
    - ❑ a. start at the beginning and read in order to the end.
    - ❑ b. skim to find a part that capture my attention, read that, and then find another interesting part to read.

2. I prefer to:
    - ❑ a. find out everything I can about one subject.
    - ❑ b. know bits and pieces about a lot of different subjects.

3. I remember:
    - ❑ a. the overall concept, main idea, and general information best.
    - ❑ b. facts and details best.

4. I think students should:
    - ❑ a. spend enough time in one subject area to become highly knowledgeable, then move on to another subject area.
    - ❑ b. learn about a wide variety of subjects.

5. When I am learning something new, I prefer to:
    - ❑ a. learn the overall concept or main idea first.
    - ❑ b. focus on the details, step-by-step.

6. I tend to have difficulty:
    - ❑ a. seeing the "big picture" or how everything fits together.
    - ❑ b. seeing the "little" things, or putting things in order.

7. After watching a movie, or reading a story, I usually remember:
    - ❑ a. the main idea, plot, or theme.
    - ❑ b. specific details and steps of exactly how something happened.

8. When I'm learning something that's interesting, I usually:
    - ❑ a. get the overall concept and like to know why it's important.
    - ❑ b. like going into more detail and knowing what comes next.

9. When reading a magazine, I like to:
    - ❑ a. flip through the whole thing and get a general idea of what it's all about.
    - ❑ b. find an interesting article or story to read, then find another one.

10. When I think about the last time I went somewhere and really had fun, I remember:
    - ❑ a. the overall experience in general.
    - ❑ b. specific incidents of what happened first, then next, and so on...

Now, on the next page, you'll discover what your score means and how to use it for your advantage.

Big Chunk-Little Chunk Scoring and Explanations

- *"a" Answers*

  If most of your answers were letter "a" then that suggests that you prefer to learn the overall concept of things. You want to see the big picture and like to figure out how things relate. It takes real concentration for you to pick up details and things like that. Instead you find the main idea of what is happening. You learn things in big chunks.

- *"b" Answers*

  If more of these answers are chosen, this indicate that you probably pay close attention to the details. You understand how things go in sequence. You notice, hear, and catch the "little" things. It takes some focus and precision for you to see the big picture. You learn through understanding the little chunks of information.

Suggestion:
Train yourself by starting with your own style and then increase your capacity to learn both ways. If you tend to pay attention to details, flip the script and visualize the BIG picture for a moment each day. If you usually look at the whole picture, step out of character and take a glance at the details. This way, you get more of what you really want in less time. Now, who would not like to experience that?

c. Three Important Questions to Ask During a Parent-Teacher-Student Conference

1. Kids learn differently. What learning approach is best for me to use with my child at home?
2. What can I do to incorporate his learning style when he studies?
3. What are some things the school is doing that is working, that I can do at home?

Other Important Questions

- If *that* doesn't work, what else could be tried?
- David feels inadequate and has lost his enthusiasm for learning. What do you suppose could have made him feel this way? What can the school do to help?
- What can we do that we have not done before?
- Does it make sense to continue something that is not working?
- How should a child respond if a teacher yells at her?
- I apologize for my ignorance. Will you please explain that in simple words?
- I want my child to get the best education possible. What can he do? What can I do? What will the school do?

TLC TIP:
Have your child attend the conference or a portion. During this time, your child will interview the teacher (see form on the next page) to find out what he or she can do to improve her/his grades.

Variation:
Your child can also use this form at the beginning of each semester, for each of his teachers, or anytime he wants an easier way to find out what makes a teacher give good grades.

d. Ask The Teacher

In order to help your child get better grades easier, have him/her interview the teacher. Ask the following questions. Place a check on the behavior, or, fill in what he/she says.

Teacher's Name_____

What are the three **most important** things that I need to do in order to get an "A" in this class.

_____Listen when the teacher is talking.

_____Write so that the teacher can read it.

_____Allow others to complete their work.

_____Complete all of my assignments.   (With at least _____% accuracy)

_____Come to school everyday.

_____Use appropriate language.

Other:

_____

_____

Other Important Questions:

1. When you are teaching, how do you know when a student "gets it"?
2. What's the best thing to do if I need help and you are busy?
3. How do you know when you are respected?

e. Very Helpful Websites

http://star.cde.ca.gov/
Lifeimprovementinc.com
superachievement.net
http://www.ed.gov/pubs/SchlProj/prof6.html
http://www.bridges4kids.org/BBR.html
www.drkswiggins.com
Theachievementgroupinc.com

f. Other Books by This Author

Creative Solutions to Academic Barriers
Test-Taking Tactics – Helping Your Student Test Better
Straight Up! Every Teens Guide to Success
Standards-Based Strategies For Skyrocketing Success-*An Easy Interactive Curriculum Designed to Help Students Achieve Success Faster and More Enjoyably.*

g. Contact Information

selinajackson@sbcglobal.net

Index

Printed in the United States
R1764800002BA/R17648PG38014LVSX00006BA/10-60